THE POCKET LIBRARY OF GREAT ART

1. PISSARRO. Saint Martin Pig Market. *1886. Pencil*
Collection John Rewald, New York

FRENCH IMPRESSIONISTS

AND THEIR CIRCLE

text by
HERMAN J. WECHSLER

published by HARRY N. ABRAMS, INC., *in association with* POCKET BOOKS, INC., *New York*

FIRST PRINTING

2. MONET. Port of Touques near Honfleur. *1870*. *Conté crayon*
Wildenstein and Co., New York

TODAY THE TERM IMPRESSIONISM has not only
found its way into the language of critic and lay-
man alike, but it immediately evokes images of a
series of brilliant canvases by painters who are now
being called "traditional"—sometimes "old masters"!
Yet less than one hundred years ago, the efforts of
these same artists were considered "outlandish" and
"insults to the painter's craft."

In the year 1874, a group of French painters who
had had their offerings systematically rejected by the
jury of the official Salon, arranged their own exhibit

on the vacated premises of the photographer Nadar, situated on one of Paris' busiest thoroughfares. Some thirty artists showed their wares, among them being Degas, Renoir, Monet, Pissarro, Cézanne, Sisley, Berthe Morisot. Manet, although sympathetic to the group's activity, did not exhibit on this occasion.

The public and critics came to the humble quarters, paid a modest entrance fee, and experienced varied sensations. Some were honestly bewildered, others infuriated—the majority simply amused. Cézanne bore the brunt of the strongest insults, but it was one of Monet's pictures, entitled *Impression—Sunrise,* which gave the movement and the group its name, for a wit among the critics seized upon this title and labeled all the pictures shown as "impressionistic." Thus the word "impressionism," used first as a term of derision, was adopted by the very victims of this mockery as a label for their group and a proud banner for their rebellion. Their revolt was against the official art of the Salon, the neo-classicism of the Academy, the elaborate set of ironclad rules which enslaved most of the artists of the day.

But the Impressionists were not alone in their century's rebellion. The great Ingres had thought of himself as a "revolutionary"; Courbet, with his stark realism, offended the official school; Delacroix had already deeply shocked the academicians by his "romantic" pictures; and Daumier went his quiet way to record and ennoble the everyday activity of the French bourgeoisie, ignoring the Greeks and Romans, except

3. RENOIR. Sketch for the Misses Lerolle. *1890. Conté crayon
Collection Durand-Ruel, Paris*

4. RENOIR. Drawing for L'Assomoir. *1877-78. Ink. Collection John Nic*

s Brown, Providence, R. 1.

in such instances as he chose to satirize their glory.

Here, then, is a group of men and women of varying temperaments, dispositions, nationalities, and talents, linked together in a common effort to fight officialdom, to experiment with new forms and theories, to express themselves freely in a manner unhampered by rules and traditions. The artists presented in the following pages did not all give themselves completely and wholeheartedly to the tenets and practices of Impressionism. Only two or three among them clung tenaciously to its theories in their purest form. Such were Sisley, Pissarro, and Monet. But the other artists who are dealt with in this book were at some time close enough to the movement to warrant their being linked to the group. Cézanne and Van Gogh went through an Impressionistic phase. Seurat's "pointillism" could not have come into being without the prior experiment. Manet, Degas, and Renoir produced some unforgettable canvases according to its formulae, and later evolved their personal styles. Gauguin, a banker and amateur painter, first met members of the group in nocturnal café gatherings, became one of the first collectors of their canvases, and when he finally gave up business to paint professionally, was, of course, influenced by their teachings.

What, then, was the nature of this rebellion of the Impressionists, and what made their revolt so important a step in art history?

Let us consider first their choice of subject matter

5. SISLEY. View of Moret. 1892. Ink. Courtesy F.A.R. Gallery, New York

and their new attitude towards the contemporary world. Forgotten, or at least ignored, were the gods and goddesses of classical mythology and their fabled adventures. Sometimes Renoir would label a nude *Diana* or *Venus,* to win her admission to the Salon. Actually she was a healthy, full-bodied French girl who had consented to pose for him. Ignored, too, were the battle scenes, the portraits of national heroes, the historical panoramas of the more traditionally-minded artists. These painters began to look with unprejudiced eyes at the bustling life around them; they painted—as they saw them—the cafés and their habitués, prostitutes, vagabonds, drunkards, the middle-class business man. Influenced by the new art of the camera, they painted what we now call "candid" views—a moment of life seized and recorded—a man lifting a drink to his lips, a woman entering a doorway. People are often depicted moving *into* or *out of* the canvas, their bodies or faces cut off by the limiting frame. It is as though the artist had accidentally come upon some scene which intrigued him and had quickly "caught it" and noted it down. Often, of course, this was carefully "worked up" at the studio, but the notes, written or remembered, were made at the moment of observation. Also, the trivial was accepted as subject matter—a single dead fish on a platter, a few pieces of fruit, a spray of flowers. These men, too, sought for inspiration and for ideas everywhere—from the Japanese print, exotic native carvings, tiles and ceramics from the Near and Far

6. GAUGUIN. Tahitian Girl Crouching. *About 1892. Pencil*
   The Art Institute of Chicago

East, objects which we often see in the backgrounds of their pictures.

But in the realm of color, the changes seemed more extreme to the old guard, for the Impressionists, often accused of being mere "scientists," investigated the new laws of optics, "broke up" their colors, and juxtaposed dashes and blobs of paint so that the mixture was made in the eye of the observer and not blended on the palette. The painter's paraphernalia was carried out to the streets and fields, where the effect of sunlight was studied systematically. Monet painted the same scene over and over again, demonstrating how different was the aspect of the same object under changing conditions of light. He made his famous experiments with the façade of Rouen Cathedral; groups of haystacks in a field and the lily ponds of his own home also served as subject matter.

These are but a few of Impressionism's contributions. In the pages which follow, mention will be made of others. But the reader, if he has been moved by the pictures included in this book—or made curious by the foregoing paragraphs—is urged to seek out other pictures by these artists and the many thoughtful texts by the writers on Impressionism.

7. CASSATT. Little Girl with Dog. *About 1904. Pastel*
Knoedler Galleries, New York

8. PISSARRO. Portrait of Paul Cézanne. *1874. Etching*
Collection John Rewald, New York

COLOR PLATES

PLATE 9

Edouard Manet (1832-1883)

BOATING AT ARGENTEUIL

Museum of Fine Arts, Tournai, Belgium

Painted in 1874   Oil, 48⅝ x 51⅝"

In the summer of 1874, Monet, Renoir, and Manet were together at Argenteuil on the Seine near Paris and painted several portraits of each other with their families and friends. This picture of Claude Monet and his wife is one of the most vivid and suggests Manet's close ties with the Impressionists, even though he always refused to exhibit with them. From this date Manet's paintings become more and more marked by the broken color and bright palette of the work of his associates. Outdoor themes, unusual in his early paintings, become much more common, and his attitude is gayer and more carefree.

PLATE 10

Edgar Degas (1834-1917)

CAFE-CONCERT: THE SONG OF THE DOG

Collection Horace Havemeyer, New York

Painted 1875-77   *Gouache and pastel, 21⅝ x 17¾"*

This painting is a brilliant impression of a moment; it is handled with a freedom that could only be called "impressionistic"; and yet it is not strictly an Impressionist painting. Although he associated with the Impressionists and exhibited in all but one of their eight shows, Degas always remained something of a stubborn traditionalist. He did not follow them in their loose drawing and atmospheric coloring, and more than once he expressed a frank distaste for "out-of-door" landscape painting, so central to the art of Monet, Sisley, Renoir, and Pissarro. If the term Impressionism can include psychological elements, however, then no one surpassed Degas in the ability to render momentary impressions of candid human gestures and movements. Here, under a dazzle of lights, he rapidly sets down in flowing brush strokes one of those vivid entertainment spectacles that so intrigued him.

PLATE 11

Pierre Auguste Renoir (1841-1919)

HER FIRST EVENING OUT

Tate Gallery, London

Painted about 1880   *Oil, 25½ x 19¾"*

Except for this eager and wide-eyed girl, the canvas
is a hubbub of movement and implied sound. Renoir's
flashing brush strokes convey the dazzle of Paris life
as it impresses the girl. In the boldest and simplest
manner he weaves the picture into a unity through
such devices as the repeat of the front contours of the
girl's jacket in the curve of the partition behind her,
and in the variation of this line in her back. The color
is held down in general value and intensity, but it is
altogether Renoiresque in its rich invention.

Plate 12. PISSARRO. PATH AT PONTOISE *(commentary follows color*

section)

PLATE 13

Claude Monet (1840-1926)

SUNFLOWERS

The Metropolitan Museum of Art, New York

Painted in 1881   *Oil, 39¾ x 32"*

Monet was the most consistent member of the Impressionist group and carried their practices to their most radical conclusion. In his late canvases he dissolved forms completely in colored mists. Unlike other Impressionists, he never chafed against formlessness or tried to revive architectural elements in his compositions.

In this canvas Monet is primarily interested in rendering the effects of light on form and impregnating the surrounding atmosphere with color. Yet the individual forms still stand out distinctly from this atmosphere.

PLATE I 4

Camille Pissarro (1830-1903)

THE APPLE PICKERS

Collection William B. Jaffe, New York

Painted in 1881   Oil, 25⅝ x 21¼"

Camille Pissarro might very well be called the "elder statesman" of the Impressionist group. A man of great dignity and restraint, he won the admiration of his fellow artists who listened to his learned and articulate exposition of art theories when they gathered nightly at the favored Paris cafés. Mary Cassatt, a disciple, once commented that Camille was so great a teacher "that he could have taught stones to draw correctly."

For Pissarro the countryside was a constant source of inspiration. The homely, rustic scene here, bathed in cool, blue-green light, is executed with the minute color dots, or "pointillism," of his later technique. It reveals the same serenity and love of nature that are reflected in his beautiful letters to his son Lucien.

portion of plate 15 (open page opposite)

PLATE 15

Georges Seurat (1859-1891)

AN AFTERNOON AT LA GRANDE JATTE

The Metropolitan Museum of Art, New York

Painted in 1884   Oil, 27¾ x 41"

La Grande Jatte, an island park in the Seine on the
outskirts of Paris, was a favorite place for Sunday
afternoon strolls and outdoor recreation. It is here
recorded in a sketch made for Seurat's more formal
and intricately planned canvas owned by The Art
Institute of Chicago. The sketch combines Impressionist innovations and subject matter with Seurat's
own disciplined method, and catches the atmosphere
of a summer afternoon.

Seurat continued the Impressionists' study of color
on a scientific basis and devised a new method of
painting known as "pointillism." He placed spots of
color next to each other on the canvas so that from
a distance of several feet the forms and local colors
of the composition came into focus. This method en-
abled him to create the shimmering effect—so striking
here—of colored objects seen in sunlight and shadow.

PLATE 16

Berthe Morisot (1841-1895)

IN THE DINING ROOM

National Gallery of Art, Washington, D. C.
(Chester Dale Collection)

Painted 1881-83   Oil, 24¼ x 19¾"

A charming and accomplished woman, Berthe Morisot managed to combine successfully the roles of painter, mother, and hostess. She was dedicated to her art and yet raised a family with her husband, Eugène, brother of the painter Edouard Manet. For the rebel group of Impressionists, with whom she worked side by side, her home provided a genteel social atmosphere where they were always welcome. The poet Paul Valéry said of her, "She lives her painting and she paints her life," and he compared her work to "the diary of a woman who expresses herself by color and drawing." Berthe Morisot contributed her own unique artistic qualities to Impressionism—a silvery delicacy of tone and a certain feminine charm in her choice and handling of everyday subject matter.

PLATE 17

Edgar Degas (1834-1917)

TWO LAUNDRESSES

The Louvre, Paris

Painted about 1884   Oil, 29⅞ x 32¼"

Degas anticipated the modern candid camera by many years. Here his models are caught in the midst of their gestures, unposed and unaware of being observed. The artist has dared to represent one figure stretching and yawning and the other absorbed in her ironing. Such commonplace incidents were absent from painting until the Impressionists; and Degas was perhaps unique in finding an almost classical form to express so homely a scene from everyday life. For although the painting has an air of utter naturalness, it has been meticulously composed. The play of movement and counter-movement and the careful patterning of color declare Degas' traditional ties and classical thoroughness.

Plate *18*. SISLEY. ROAD TO LOUVECIENNES (*commentary follows colo.*

te section)

PLATE 19

Paul Cézanne (1839-1906)

CHESTNUT TREES AT THE JAS DE BOUFFAN

The Minneapolis Institute of Arts

Painted 1885-87   Oil, 28¾ x 36¼"

Cézanne belongs with the Impressionists, not primarily because of his adherence to their theories, but because he was one of the rebels who participated in their first exhibitions. By the time he painted *Chestnut Trees* Cézanne had turned away from Impressionist practices. Rather than striving only for evanescent effects of light which dissolve forms, he used vivid color to create an "Impressionism of forms," evoking, through shifting planes, sensations of solidity and depth in space. In solitude in the south of France this dedicated hermit-artist passed his last years painting his new vision of nature, rarely satisfied with results. His grandiose experiment, appreciated by few in his lifetime, revolutionized modern art.

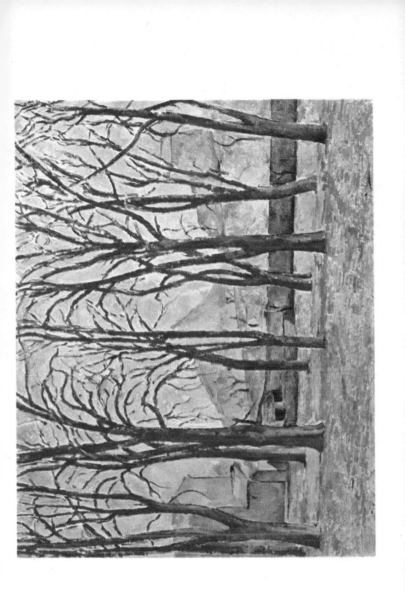

portion of plate 20 (open page opposite)

PLATE 20

Pierre Auguste Renoir (1841-1919)

MADAME CHARPENTIER AND HER CHILDREN

The Metropolitan Museum of Art, New York

Painted in 1878   Oil, 60½ x 74⅞"

This portrait is, in a sense, the result of a wonderfully successful compromise between the requirements of society portraiture and the personal vision of the artist. As a charming revelation of a particular woman and her family—Madame Charpentier was one of the most celebrated Parisian hostesses—of her personality and the quality of her home, this picture is an unqualified success, and was so regarded when it was shown in the Salon of 1879. But it is also successful as a Renoir: full of grace and freshness, and arranged with a freedom rather unusual in a picture in which the various elements are not the choice of the artist at liberty in his own studio.

PLATE 21

Paul Cézanne (1839-1906)

SELF-PORTRAIT WITH PALETTE

Collection the Artist's Family, Paris

Painted 1885-87   *Oil, 36¼ x 28¾"*

Cézanne painted many self-portraits, all of them
severe, immobile. As psychological interpretations they
are most impersonal. As abstract arrangements of form
and color they have been acclaimed supreme by critics,
on a level with the greatest classical art of the past.
Here Cézanne employs the light palette and flecking
brush strokes of the Impressionists. But he uses them
to create a figure in space which has the purity of
volume and grave nobility of French architectural
sculpture of the Gothic period. At the same time, the
flatness of his design and its abstract severity suggest
the Cubists; these last qualities earned for Cézanne
the title "father of modern art."

PLATE 22

Vincent van Gogh (1853-1890)

THE NIGHT CAFE

Collection Stephen C. Clark, New York

Painted in 1888 Oil, 27½ x 35"

After failing as a preacher and a picture dealer, Van Gogh settled upon a career of painting. In his brother Theo, a Paris art dealer, he found a lifelong good angel who supported him financially and kept Vincent's sagging spirits up. Theo brought him to Paris and introduced him to the Impressionist circle whose brilliant colors and fresh angles of vision transformed his art from the somberness and conservatism of his Dutch period. The new impact of the Impressionist palette is apparent in *The Night Café*. Van Gogh has gone beyond his contemporaries, however, even while retaining their freedom; he has given color a new emotional and personal impact. The artist described the disturbing symbolism of this painting thus: "I have tried to express the terrible passions of humanity by means of red and green."

PLATE 23

Vincent van Gogh (1853-1890)

WHEAT FIELD WITH CYPRESSES

Tate Gallery, London

Painted in 1889   *Oil, 28½ x 36"*

This painting was done at Saint-Rémy under the impact of the southern sunlight, which had such a liberating effect on Van Gogh's art. To his brother Theo he had written ecstatically upon his first contact with the south, "Behold the kingdom of light! How wonderful is the golden sun!" The south inspired countless landscapes, none more rhapsodic than this one. Van Gogh's lyrical brush sweeps up nature in the rhythm of his own powerful emotion until field, trees, mountains, and clouds become almost abstract, free-flowing forms. These coiling and fantastic shapes suggest how far Vincent's stormy feelings carried him beyond the relatively impersonal commentaries on nature which the Impressionists painted.

portion of plate 24 (open page opposite)

PLATE 24

Edouard Manet (1832-1883)

A BAR AT THE FOLIES-BERGERE

Courtauld Institute of Art, London

Painted in 1881   *Oil, 37¾ x 50"*

This painting was exhibited in the official Salon of 1882, a year before Manet's death. His work by then no longer shocked or bewildered a public that had become accustomed to his revolutionary treatment of realism and Impressionistic handling. But it still did not arouse very great enthusiasm. The brilliant virtuosity of Manet's brush, his rich and subtle observation of a contemporary subject, and the delicate color harmonies of this ambitious canvas were largely overlooked. Although he was nominated *Chevalier de la Légion d'Honneur* the same year, he could write bitterly, "Now it is too late to compensate for twenty years' lack of success."

PLATE 25

Claude Monet (1840-1926)

CANAL AT ZAANDAM

Wildenstein and Co., New York

Painted in 1871   *Oil, 16⅝ x 28¾"*

At the end of the Franco-Prussian war Monet went briefly to Holland and painted there for several months. He was attracted by the openness of the landscape, the immensity of sky, and the picturesque windmills that seemed to grow out of the water. The reflections of light on water, a recurrent theme in early Impressionist paintings, also no doubt intrigued him. The mobile water surfaces broke up light into varicolored hues, and the dancing effects may even have suggested to the Impressionists those vibrant little brush strokes so characteristic of their work.

PLATE 26

Henri de Toulouse-Lautrec (1864-1901)

PORTRAIT OF A LADY IN RED

Collection Mrs. Albert D. Lasker, New York

Painted in 1890   *Oil, 28¾ x 16"*

This picture was painted in the period when Lautrec was on the threshold of his mature style, but still under the spell of the Impressionists. Although he never exhibited with the group, he was affected by their technique and aims. Here the freedom of handling and the interest in rendering light and the atmosphere surrounding his figure suggest his debt to Impressionist methods. His emphasis on the human and psychological aspects of the subject, however, place him in another generation and prefigure later developments in his art.

PLATE 27

Paul Gauguin (1848-1903)

IA ORANA MARIA

(We Greet Thee, Mary)

The Metropolitan Museum of Art, New York
(Bequest of Samuel A. Lewisohn)

Painted in 1891   Oil, 44¾ x 34½"

Gauguin was a prosperous stockbroker, a married man, and a Sunday painter when in 1883 he dramatically abandoned career and family to dedicate himself wholly to painting. His restless spirit drove him to Brittany where he established a colony of artists, to Arles where he painted with Van Gogh, and finally to the South Seas. In the primitive Eden of Tahiti he found his spiritual home.

After exhibiting with the Impressionists in the early eighties and assimilating their innovations, Gauguin developed a radically new style that emphasized strong outlines and brilliant, ornamental color. *Ia Orana Maria* is one of his few religious paintings. It is Christian in feeling even while it exploits the exotic elements that had drawn Gauguin to Tahiti: the beauty of its women, the lush, colorful vegetation, and the mysticism of the natives.

IA ORANA MARIA

PLATE 28

Mary Cassatt (1855-1926)

MOTHER AND CHILD

The Metropolitan Museum of Art, New York

Painted about 1905   Oil, 36½ x 29"

Mary Cassatt and Berthe Morisot were the only two
women to exhibit with the Impressionists; and Miss
Cassatt was the only American member of the group.
Although never actually a pupil of Degas, she was one
of the few artists welcome in his studio and learned
much from him. She shared with Degas his need to
intellectualize emotions in clear, objective forms and
his emphasis on draftsmanship. To this she added a
sentiment of her own, concentrating on more intimate
and tender themes like this one of motherhood. Her
directness and boldly simplified color arrangements
gave a fresh American flavor to Impressionist work.

Camille Pissarro (1830-1903)

PATH AT PONTOISE

Wildenstein and Co., New York

Painted 1869-70   Oil, 20½ x 32"

Though Pissarro, with Monet and Sisley, found refuge in England during the Franco-Prussian war, he did not escape its tragedy. His studio at Louveciennes was ransacked by the Germans and only forty of the fifteen hundred canvases he left behind were recovered. This is one of the few that survived.

Although there are Impressionist effects in the colored shadows, this painting is still early in style and suggests the work of Corot, the master Pissarro revered. Only after his trip to England did Pissarro become a full-fledged Impressionist, pursuing fugitive effects of light with bright, broken colors. It may have been the impact of the English landscape painting of Constable, Turner, and Gainsborough, which the Impressionists came to appreciate while in England, that encouraged them to proceed with their radical new vision.

Alfred Sisley (1839-1899)

ROAD TO LOUVECIENNES

Wildenstein and Co., New York

Painted in 1873   Oil, 15 x 21⅝"

Alfred Sisley, a veteran of the original Impressionist group and its only English member, did not receive recognition or honor during his lifetime and died in poverty, tortured by cancer of the throat. But the bitterness which he came to feel for life and humanity never found expression in his tender and poetic landscapes of the countryside around Paris. A fellow-student of Renoir and Monet at the studio of Gleyre, he, too, rebelled against academic subjects and turned to "open-air" painting. Forests, riverbanks, bridges, avenues of trees, distant views of towns, observed in summer and winter, all served as subjects for Sisley, whose art remained lyrical despite personal suffering.

29. MANET. A Café Interior. *1869. Pen and brush. Fogg Museum, Cambridge (Sachs Coll.)*

30. MANET. Lola de Valence. *1861 62. Ink, pencil, and gouache*
Fogg Art Museum, Cambridge, Mass.

31. SEURAT. The Artist's Mother. *About 1883. Conté crayon*
Museum of Modern Art, New York (Lillie P. Bliss Collection)

32. SEURAT. Heads of Men. *About 1885. Ink*
Wildenstein and Co., New York

33. DEGAS. Lady with a Fan. *1872. Pencil and colored crayon*
    Private collection, New York

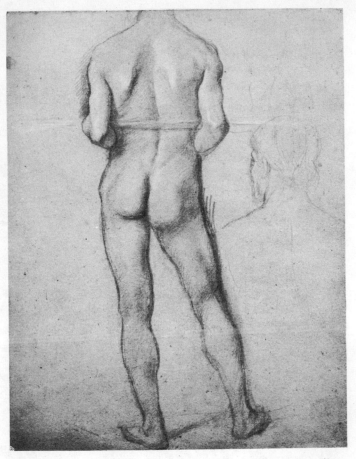

34. DEGAS. Study for Young Spartans Exercising. *1860. Pencil*
Courtesy Durand-Ruel, Paris

35. VAN GOGH. Fishing Boats at Saintes-Maries. *1888. Ink. Collection*

36. VAN GOGH. Zouave. *1888. Ink*
Collection Mr. and Mrs. J. K. Thannhauser, New York

37. TOULOUSE-LAUTREC. Réjane and Galipaux. *Lithograph*
1894. Collection Ludwig Charell, New York

38. CEZANNE. Woodland Scene. *1895-1900. Water color*
Private collection, New York

39. CEZANNE. Putto. *1885-90. Pencil*
Collection Mr. and Mrs. Harry N. Abrams, New York

1862   Monet, Renoir, and Sisley meet at Gleyre's studio, Ecole des Beaux-Arts, Paris.

1874   First group exhibition of the *Societé anonyme des artistes, peintres, sculpteurs, graveurs, etc.* at Nadar's studio. The thirty artists exhibiting are dubbed "Impressionists" by hostile press.

1875   Group auction sale at Hôtel Drouot; police are summoned to quell violent demonstrations.

1876–82 Further group exhibitions; number of participants declines.

1886   Eighth and final group exhibition of seventeen painters. Monet and Renoir withdraw, probably in protest against the admittance of Seurat.

SOME OPINIONS

IN NEWSPAPERS OF THE TIME

Louis Leroy, in *Charivari,* Paris, 1874: "Oh, it was indeed a strenuous day when I ventured into the first exhibition on the boulevard des Capucines in the company of M. Joseph Vincent, landscape painter, pupil of Bertin, recipient of medals and decorations under several governments! The rash man had come there without suspecting anything; he thought he would see the kind of painting one sees everywhere, good and bad, rather bad than good, but not hostile to good artistic manners, to devotion to form and respect for the masters. Oh, form! Oh, the masters! We don't want them any more, my poor fellow! We've changed all that."

Albert Wolff, in *Le Figaro*, Paris, 1876: "At Durand-Ruel's there has just opened an exhibition of so-called painting. The inoffensive passer-by, attracted by the flags that decorate the facade, goes in, and a ruthless spectacle is offered to his dismayed eyes: five or six lunatics—among them a woman—a group of unfortunate creatures stricken with the mania of ambition have met there to exhibit their works. . . . It is a frightening spectacle of human vanity gone astray to the point of madness. Try to make M. Pissarro understand that trees are not violet, that the sky is not the color of fresh butter, that in no country do we see the things he paints and that no intelligence can accept such aberrations! Try indeed to make M. Degas see reason; tell him that in art there are certain qualities called drawing, color, execution, control, and he will laugh in your face and treat you as a reactionary. Or try to explain to M. Renoir that a woman's torso is not a mass of flesh in the process of decomposition with green and violet spots which denote the state of complete putrefaction of a corpse."

Le Pays, Paris, 1877: "It appertains to madness; it is a deliberate excursion into the realm of the horrible and the execrable. One might surmise that all these pictures were painted with closed eyes by the insane, who on tin palettes mixed, haphazard, the most violent colors."

SOME OTHER BOOKS ABOUT
THE FRENCH IMPRESSIONISTS

Theodore Duret. *Manet and the French Impressionists.*
  Philadelphia, Lippincott, 1910
  (Recollections by an intimate friend of many of
  the artists)
Camille Pissarro. *Letters to his Son Lucien,* edited by John
  Rewald. New York, Pantheon, 1943
John Rewald. *The History of Impressionism.* New York,
  The Museum of Modern Art, 1946
  (Authoritative history of the movement)
Lionello Venturi. *Les Archives de l'Impressionisme.* Paris
  and New York, Durand-Ruel, 1939
  (Valuable collection of letters, memoirs, reviews,
  and other documents concerning the Impressionists)
R. H. Wilenski. *Modern French Painters.* New York,
  Harcourt Brace, 1949

ACKNOWLEDGMENTS

*In a book of art, it seems particularly fitting to ac-
knowledge the work of craftsmen who contribute to its
making. The color plates were made by Litho-Art,
Inc., New York. The lithography is from the presses
of The Meehan-Tooker Co., Inc., New York and the
binding has been done by F. M. Charlton Co., New
York. The paper was made by P. H. Glatfelter & Co.,
York, Pa. Our deepest indebtedness is to the museums,
galleries, and private collectors who graciously per-
mitted the reproduction of their paintings, drawings,
and sculpture.*